It's another Quality Book from CGP

This book has been carefully written for Year 2 pupils learning science. It's full of questions and investigations designed to cover the Year 2 objectives on 'Living things and their habitats' from the latest National Curriculum.

There's also plenty of practice at 'Working Scientifically' throughout the book.

What CGP is all about

Our sole aim here at CGP is to produce the highest quality books — carefully written, immaculately presented and dangerously close to being funny.

Then we work our socks off to get them out to you — at the cheapest possible prices.

Contents

Section 1 — Alive or Dead?

What's Alive and What's Not 1
How Can You Tell What's Alive? (Mini-Project 1) 3

Section 2 — Habitats

Looking at Habitats 6
Habitats in Water 8
Extreme Habitats 10
Comparing Habitats 11
Living Together 13
Exploring Habitats (Mini-Project 2) 15

Section 3 — Food Chains

What Eats What? 18

Mixed Questions 22

Glossary 26

Answers to the questions are on the back of the Pull-out Poster in the centre of the book.

Published by CGP

Contributors
Katherine Faudemer, Rachael Marshall
With thanks to Charlotte Burrows and Amanda MacNaughton for the proofreading.

ISBN: 978 1 78294 234 4

Clipart from Corel®
Printed by Elanders Ltd, Newcastle upon Tyne.
Based on the classic CGP style created by Richard Parsons.

Text, design, layout and original illustrations © Coordination Group Publications Ltd. (CGP) 2014
All rights reserved.

Photocopying this book is not permitted, even if you have a CLA licence.
Extra copies are available from CGP with next day delivery • 0800 1712 712 • www.cgpbooks.co.uk

Section 1 — Alive or Dead?

What's Alive and What's Not

Some things are alive. Some things are dead. Some things have never been alive.

1. Circle the things that are **alive**. You should circle **two** things.

2. Here is a plant in a pot.

   Circle the correct words in **bold**.

   The plant is **alive / dead**.

   The wood chippings **have never been alive / are dead**.

   The plastic pot **has never been alive / is dead**.

What's Alive and What's Not

3. Circle the thing that **used to be alive**.

the <u>leather</u> in a shoe

the <u>plastic</u> in a bottle

a <u>glass</u> of water

4. Tick (✔) to show if each of these is **alive, dead**, or **has never been alive**.

	Alive	Dead	Never Alive
seaweed growing at the beach	☐	☐	☐
a dinosaur bone	☐	☐	☐
a metal door handle	☐	☐	☐
a roast chicken	☐	☐	☐
a spider spinning a web	☐	☐	☐
a plastic bag	☐	☐	☐

INVESTIGATE

Look out of your classroom window. Can you see anything that is alive? What about things that used to be alive? What can you see that has never been alive? Which type of thing can you see the most of?

How Can You Tell What's Alive?

This project is about working out how you can tell if something is alive, dead or was never alive. You will need some coloured pencils.

Find **six** objects from around your school. Pick things from **inside** and **outside**.

1. **Draw** your objects below. Write down their **names** by your pictures.

1.	2.	3.
4.	5.	6.

2. Fill in this table to show if each object is **alive**, **dead** or was **never alive**.

Alive	Dead	Never Alive

MINI-PROJECT: How Can You Tell What's Alive?

Sarah and James are doing a similar project.
They look at the objects below.

3. Sarah and James talk about how they could decide which things are alive.
Sarah says:

You can tell if something is alive because it is warm.

Draw a **green** circle around one of the objects that **is alive** but **isn't warm**.

Draw a **red** circle around one of the objects that **is warm** but **isn't alive**.

How Can You Tell What's Alive?

This is what James says.

> You can tell if a plant is alive because it has green bits.

4. Which object shows that James is wrong? Circle your answer.

   the dog   the doorstop   the tree

5. What do all the living things have **in common**? Tick (✔) **two** boxes.

   ☐ they all smell

   ☐ they all need water

   ☐ they can all walk

   ☐ they all need sunlight

   ☐ they can all grow

   If it helps, you could put a tick by all the living things on page 4.

EXTRA PROJECT
In class, talk about how you decided which things were alive, which were dead, and which were never alive. Can you think of anything else that is the same for all living things?

Section 2 — Habitats

Looking at Habitats

A plant or animal's <u>habitat</u> is the area where it <u>lives</u>.

This is a **meadow** in Britain.

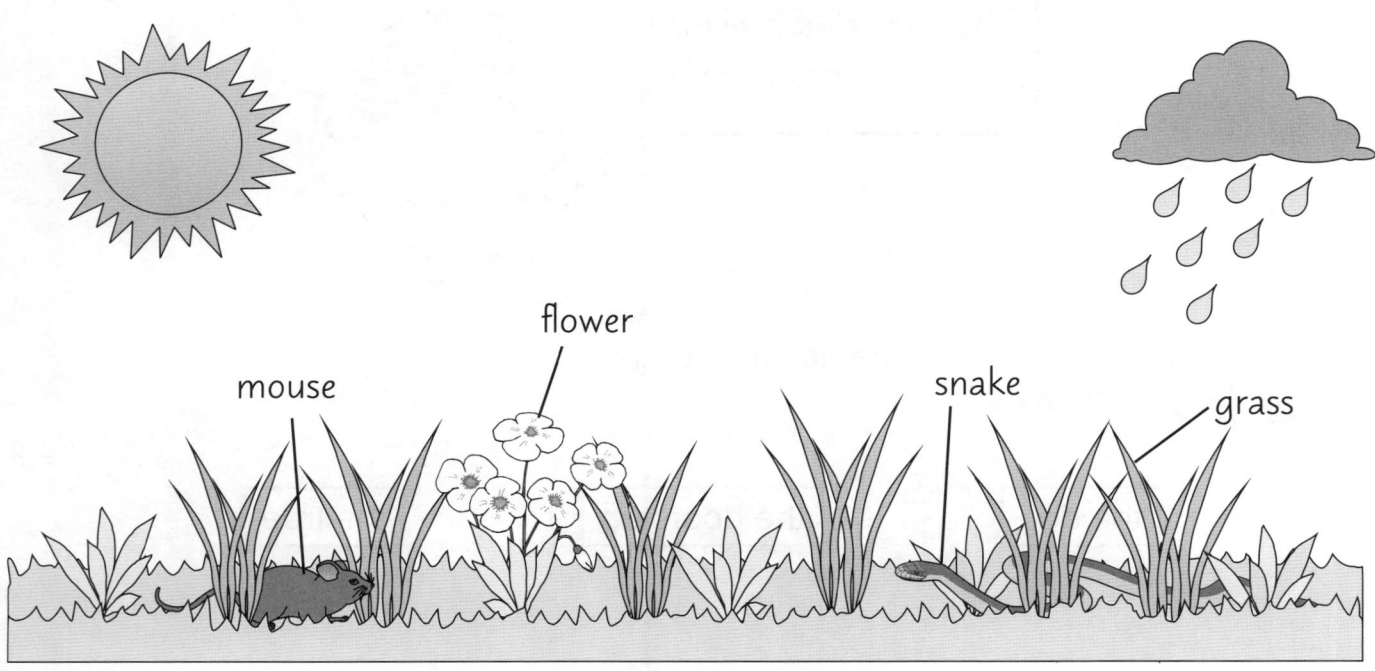

1. Cross out the wrong words in **bold**. One has been done for you.

   The meadow gets lots of rain. This helps the grass to **grow / ~~swim~~**.

   The grass can grow because there is **lots of / not much** sunlight.

   The mice can hide in the grass. It also gives them **food / nightmares**.

   The snake can eat the **grass / mice**.

2. What **other animals** could you find in this meadow? Tick (✔) **three** boxes.

   ☐ bees ☐ camels ☐ butterflies

   ☐ rabbits ☐ fish ☐ rhinos

Section 2 — Habitats

Looking at Habitats

A **wood** is another type of habitat.

3. Circle the words in **bold** that are correct. One has been done for you.

Woods have lots of **ponds / trees**.

Some trees grow **nuts / grain** that animals can eat.

The trees also give lots of animals **sunlight / shelter**.

Lots of birds use the trees to build **nests / cars**.

Animals such as foxes can eat the **birds / trees**.

A **micro-habitat** is a **small** habitat. You could find a micro-habitat under a **rock**, like this one.

4. Which words describe this micro-habitat? Tick (✔) **three** boxes.

☐ dry	☐ hot	☐ dark
☐ damp	☐ cool	☐ light

INVESTIGATE
See if you can find any micro-habitats at your school. You could look under a bush or in a pile of leaves. What sorts of animals and plants are living there?

Habitats in Water

*Habitats can be in <u>water</u>, for example, in <u>ponds</u>,
at the <u>seashore</u> or in the <u>sea</u> or the <u>ocean</u>.*

1. Finish these sentences about **ponds**.
   Use some of the words from around the picture.

Ponds are good habitats for amphibians such as ....

This is because they have wet and .... areas.

Plants such as .... grow in ponds.

These give animals somewhere to ....

2. The **seashore** is a habitat.

   Circle the things you might find at the seashore.

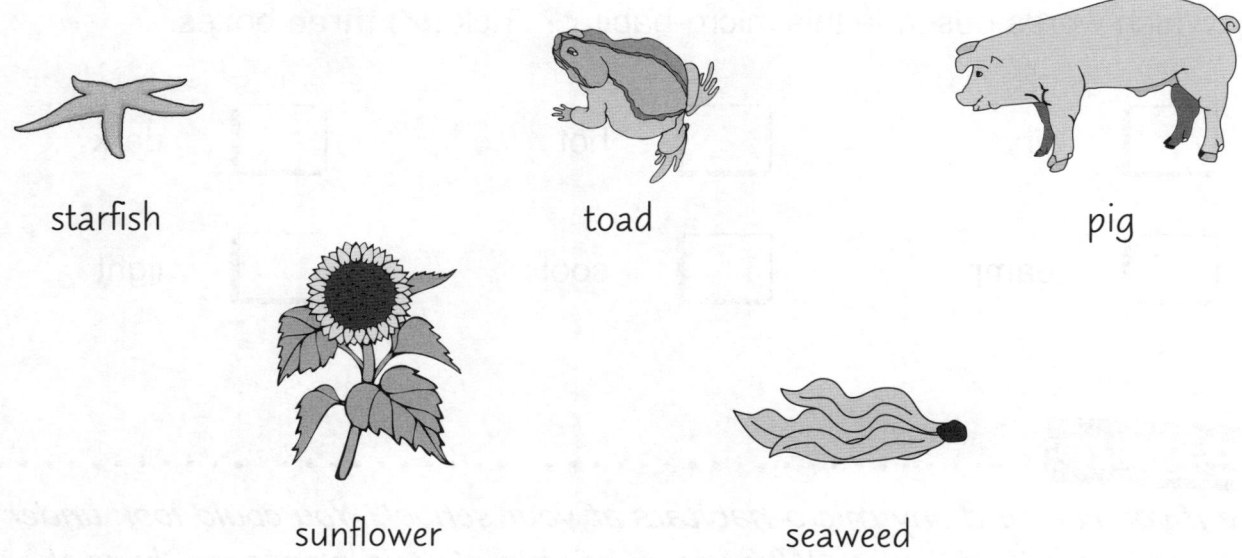

starfish   toad   pig

sunflower   seaweed

Habitats in Water

This is a habitat **under the sea**.

3. Cross out the wrong words in **bold**.

> The shallow parts of the sea get **more / less** light than the deep parts of the sea. This is where most of the plants are.
>
> Seaweed near the shore gives animals somewhere to **hide / swim**.

4. Match the picture to its name. One has been done for you.

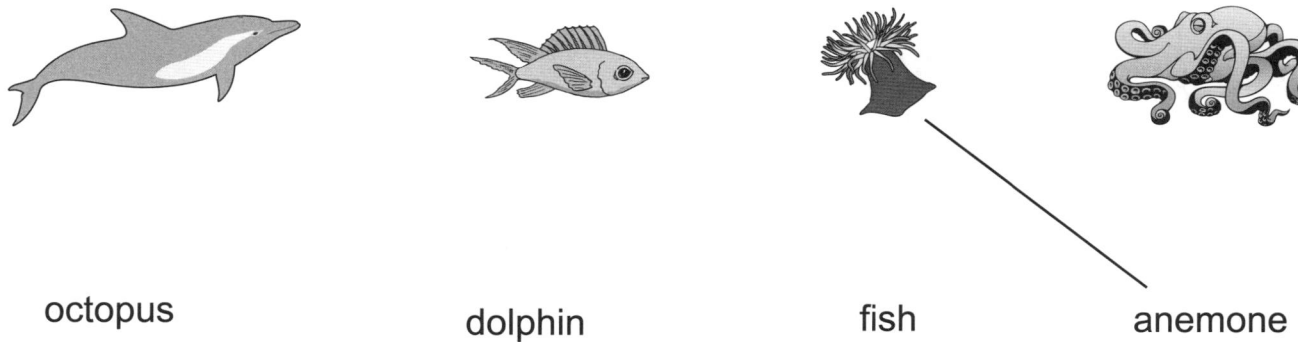

octopus   dolphin   fish   anemone

INVESTIGATE

Rivers are water habitats too. How is a river different to the sea or a pond? How is it the same? What animals do you think live in rivers? What about plants? If you don't know, use books or the Internet to help you find out.

Extreme Habitats

Some habitats are harder to live in.
We call these extreme habitats.

1. Cactuses grow in **deserts**.

   Use some of the words from the cactus to finish these sentences.

   Deserts can be very ....

   They don't have much ....

   Cactuses have .... instead of leaves.

   They have to store lots of water in their ....

   Cactus labels: spines, stem, wet, water, hot, sand

2. Polar bears live in **cold** places. They are covered in thick, white fur.

   What is a polar bear's fur for? Tick (✔) **two** boxes.

   ☐ to keep it warm

   ☐ to make it look cute

   ☐ to help it to see

   ☐ to help it hide in the snow

INVESTIGATE

What animals live in deserts? How do they survive in a desert habitat? Use books or the Internet to help you to find out. What animals do you think would not be able to live in a desert habitat? Why not?

Comparing Habitats

Comparing habitats can help you understand why different plants and animals live in different places.

Here are pictures of **two** kinds of forest.

rainforest

mountain forest

1. Use the pictures to decide if each sentence is about the **rainforest** or the **mountain forest**. Tick (✔) the correct boxes.

	rainforest	mountain forest
This is the **warmest** forest.	☐	☐
This forest has the most types of **plant**.	☐	☐
This forest has the most types of **animal**.	☐	☐

Comparing Habitats

2. Use words from the **fishing rod** to finish these sentences.

   Ponds and the sea have different .... living in them.

   This is because they are different ....

   Sea water is .... The water in ponds isn't.

   Ponds are .... than the sea.

   There are .... in the sea, but not in ponds.

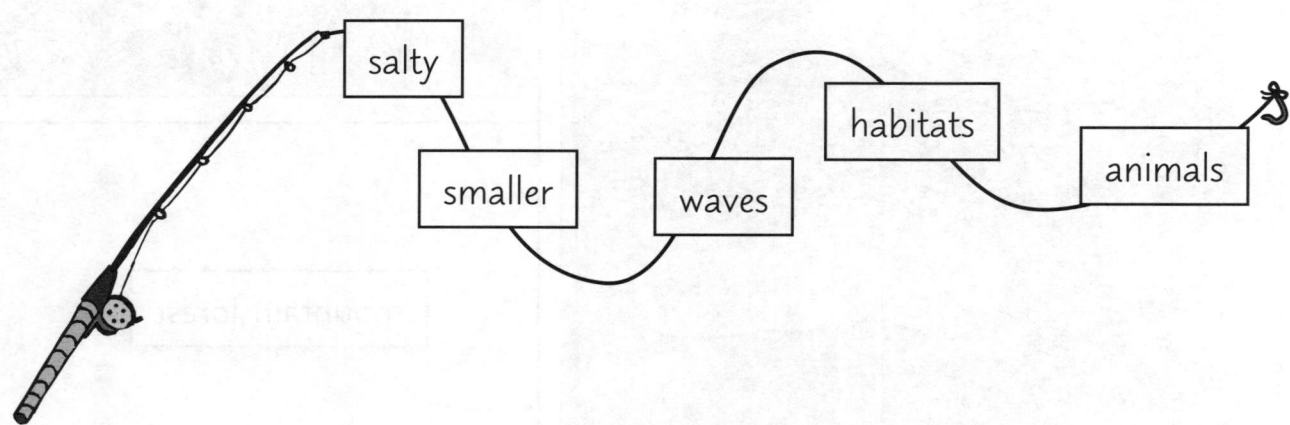

3. (Circle) the animals that might live in a **pond** habitat.

a penguin   a frog   a whale   a dragonfly

INVESTIGATE

Some animals and plants can live in more than one kind of habitat.
Can you think of any plants or animals that live in lots of different places?

PULL OUT ANSWERS AND POSTER

Answers to Y2 'Habitats'

Section 3 — Food Chains

Pages 18-21 — What Eats What?

1.

2. fox
3. flies
4. flies, blackbirds
5. These words should be crossed out: live with.
6. snails, herons
7. fish ⟶ penguins ⟶ sharks
8. leaves, squirrels, hawks, hawks
9. slugs
10. mice

Mixed Questions — Pages 22-25

1. These should be circled green: cactus, rhino, starfish.
   These should be circled red: wooden chair, leather belt, bacon.
   These should be circled blue: glass vase, keys, plastic toothbrush.
2. the place where a plant or animal lives
3.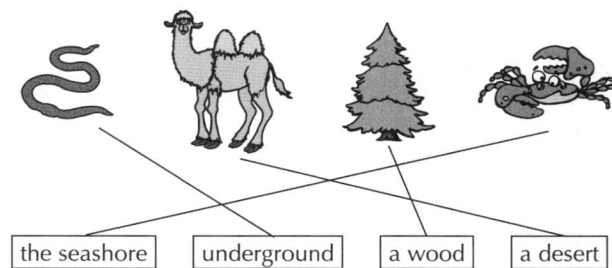
4. These should be circled: under a rock, an old log, a rock pool.
5. grass
6. to hide in when it is trying to catch gazelles
7. grass ⟶ gazelle ⟶ leopard
8. the badger, the slug, the slug, no
9. lettuce ⟶ rabbits ⟶ foxes

PULL OUT ANSWERS AND POSTER

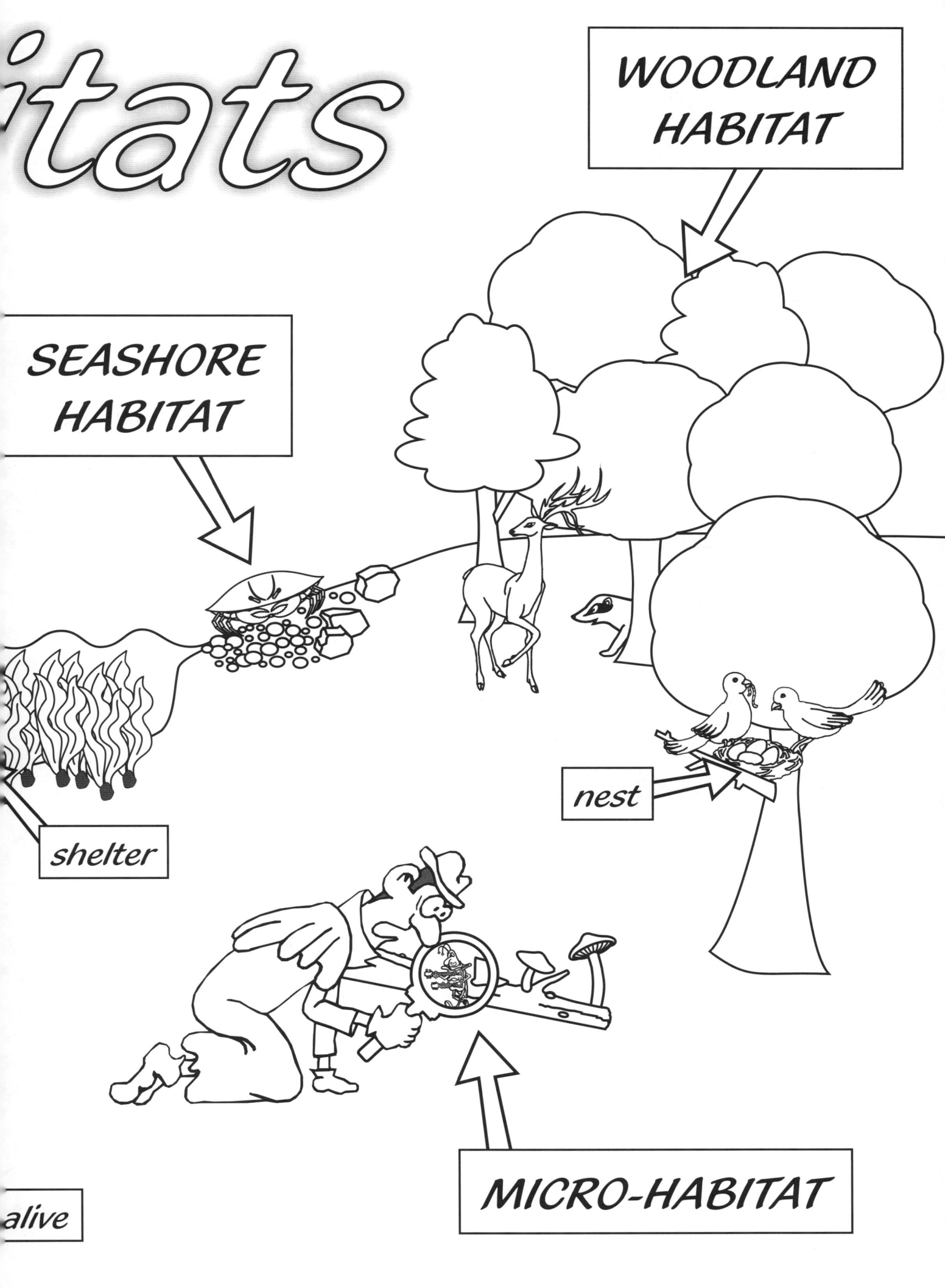

PULL OUT ANSWERS AND POSTER

Answers to Y2 'Habitats'

Section 1 — Alive or Dead?

Pages 1-2 — What's Alive and What's Not

1. The cat and the bird should be circled.
2. These words should be circled: alive, are dead, has never been alive.
3. the leather in a shoe
4. From top to bottom: alive, dead, never alive, dead, alive, never alive.

Pages 3-5 — How Can You Tell What's Alive?

1-2. This will depend on the objects you found.
3. There should be a green circle around the tree / the plant / the worm.
   There should be a red circle around the candle flame.
4. the tree
5. They all need water. They can all grow.

Section 2 — Habitats

Pages 6-7 — Looking At Habitats

1. These words should be crossed out: not much, nightmares, grass.
2. bees, butterflies, rabbits
3. These words should be circled: nuts, shelter, nests, birds.
4. dark, damp, cool

Pages 8-9 — Habitats in Water

1. frogs, dry, pond weeds, hide
2. The starfish and the seaweed should be circled.
3. These words should be crossed out: less, swim.
4.

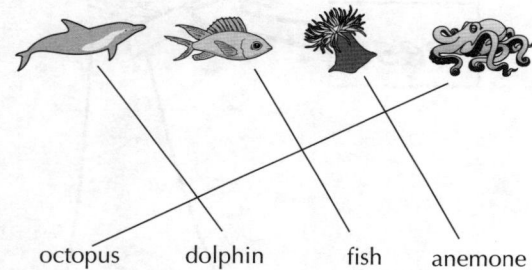

octopus   dolphin   fish   anemone

Page 10 — Extreme Habitats

1. hot, water, spines, stem
2. to keep it warm
   to help it hide in the snow

Pages 11-12 — Comparing Habitats

1. the rainforest, the rainforest, the rainforest
2. animals, habitats, salty, smaller, waves
3. The following animals should be circled: a frog, a dragonfly.

Pages 13-14 — Living Together

1. for getting twigs to make nests
   for getting food like nuts and seeds
2. in a burrow underground
3. caterpillar, mouse, sheep
4. eagle, fox, snake

Pages 15-17 — Exploring Habitats

The answers to this mini-project will depend on the micro-habitat you look at and your school field, and the weather. Using our habitats:

1. No
2. E.g.

Animal	Bird, mammal, amphibian or minibeast?
woodlouse	minibeast
spider	minibeast
millipede	minibeast
ant	minibeast
slug	minibeast

3. minibeasts
4-5. This will depend on your school field.
6. These words should be crossed out: fewer, less.
7. E.g.

Animal	Bird, mammal, amphibian or minibeast?
moth	minibeast
robin	bird
crow	bird
ladybird	minibeast
squirrel	mammal

8. From top to bottom: school field, school field, micro-habitat, micro-habitat.

Living Together

*Lots of plants and animals live together in the same habitats.
They can get some of the things they need from each other.*

1. Why are **trees** useful to **birds**?
   Tick (✔) **two** boxes.

   ☐ for getting twigs to make nests

   ☐ because trees are green

   ☐ for getting food like nuts and seeds

   ☐ because trees have roots

2. Owls need small animals to eat, like mice and **stoats**.

   stoat

   Circle the best place for a stoat to live to **hide** from owls.

   near some water

   in a burrow underground

   out in the open

Living Together

3. Circle all the animals that get their food from **plants**.

4. Lots of animals need other animals for food.
   Circle all the animals that eat **other animals**.

INVESTIGATE

- What plants and animals do you get things from? Think about the food you eat. What about the clothes you wear and the things in your house?

Exploring Habitats

In this project you'll look at habitats around your school. Be careful that you don't disturb the habitats and make sure you put everything back when you are finished.

Find a **micro-habitat** under a **log** or a **rock** around your school.

Look at the micro-habitat carefully.

1. Are there any **green plants** in your micro-habitat?
   Tick (✔) a box to show your answer.

   ☐ yes   ☐ no

2. Fill in this table to show what **animals** you see in your micro-habitat.
   Write down if each animal is a **bird**, a **mammal**, an **amphibian** or a **minibeast**.

Animal	Bird, mammal, amphibian or minibeast?

Exploring Habitats

3. Were **most** of the animals you found **birds**, **mammals**, **amphibians** or **minibeasts**? Circle your answer.

   minibeasts   birds   mammals   amphibians

   Now look at your **school field**.

4. How many **different kinds** of plant can you find? Write the number in the box.

5. Choose **two** of the plants you found. Write down their **names** and draw a **picture** of each of them below.

   If you don't know the plant's name, ask an adult or look in a book.

Plant 1	Plant 2
Name:	Name: ....

6. Cross out the words in **bold** that are **wrong**.

   There were **more / fewer** plants on the field than in the micro-habitat.

   This is because the field gets **more / less** sunlight.

Section 2 — Habitats

Exploring Habitats

7. Fill in this table to show what **animals** you see in the school field. Write down if each animal is a **bird**, a **mammal**, an **amphibian** or a **minibeast**.

Animal	Bird, mammal, amphibian or minibeast?

8. Tick (✔) to show if each sentence is about the **micro-habitat** or the **school field**.

	micro-habitat	school field
This habitat has the most **sunlight**.	☐	☐
This is the **warmest** habitat.	☐	☐
This is the **dampest** habitat.	☐	☐
This is the **most sheltered** habitat.	☐	☐

EXTRA PROJECT

Find another micro-habitat — you could look in your garden or at the park. What is this micro-habitat like? Think about things like how light it is, and what plants and animals you can see. How is it like the micro-habitat you studied at school? How is it different?

Section 3 — Food Chains

What Eats What?

Different animals eat different things.
Food chains tell you what eats what.

1. Match the **animal** on the left to the **food** it eats on the right.
   One has been done for you.

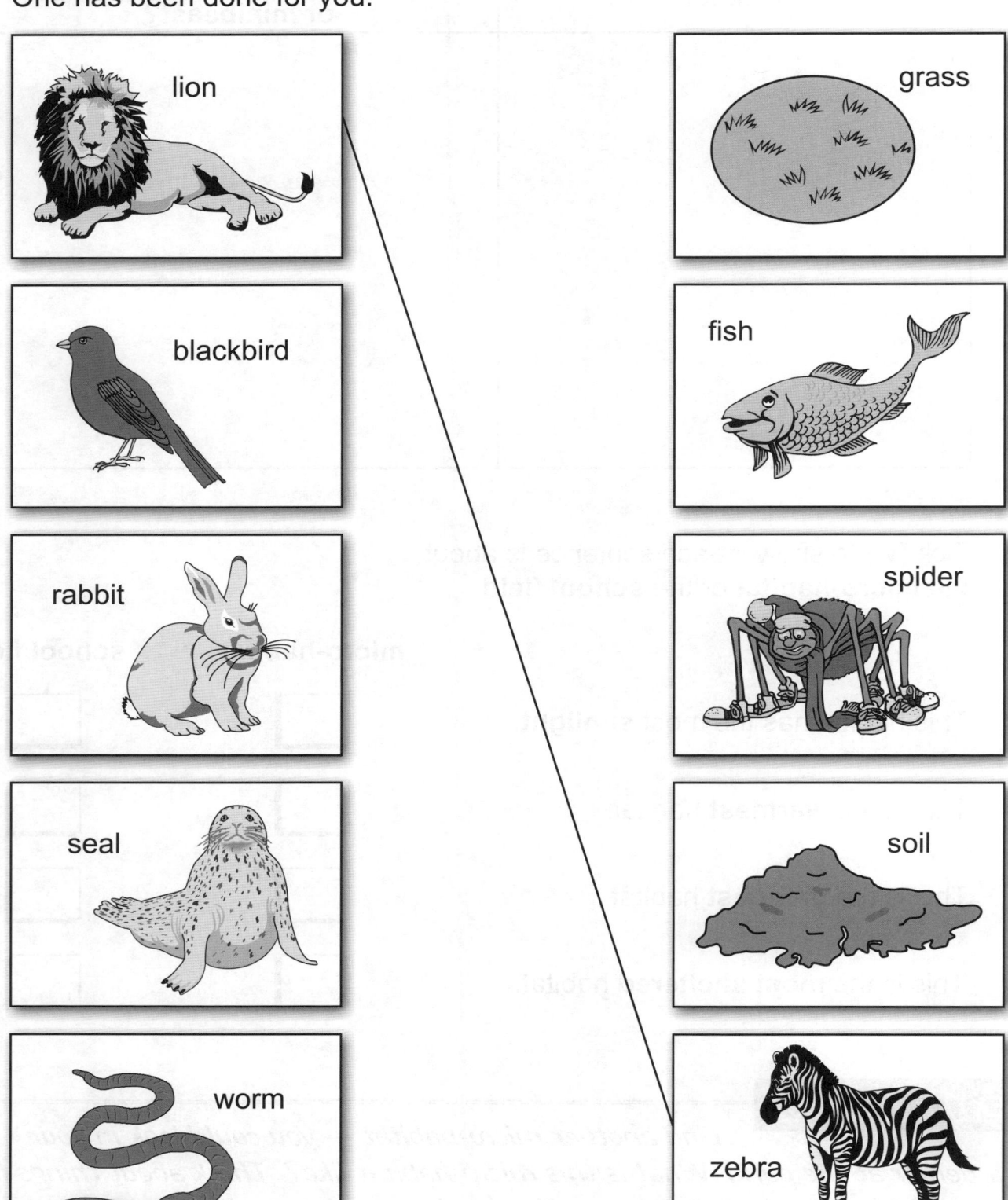

What Eats What?

2. Which animal eats **rabbits**? Circle your answer.

  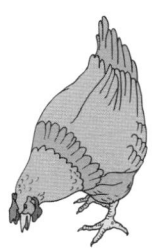 

      elephant   fox   chicken   panda

3. What does a **spider** eat? Put a tick (✔) next to your answer.

   ☐ cats   ☐ flies   ☐ birds   ☐ donkeys

4. Fill in the missing words in this **food chain** using some of the words from the box.

spiders	flies
blackbirds	rabbits

   .... ⇨ spiders ⇨ ....
         eaten by   eaten by

5. Cross out the wrong words in **bold** in this sentence.

   Food chains show which animals **eat / live with** which other animals or plants.

What Eats What?

6. Use the **food chain** to answer the questions below.

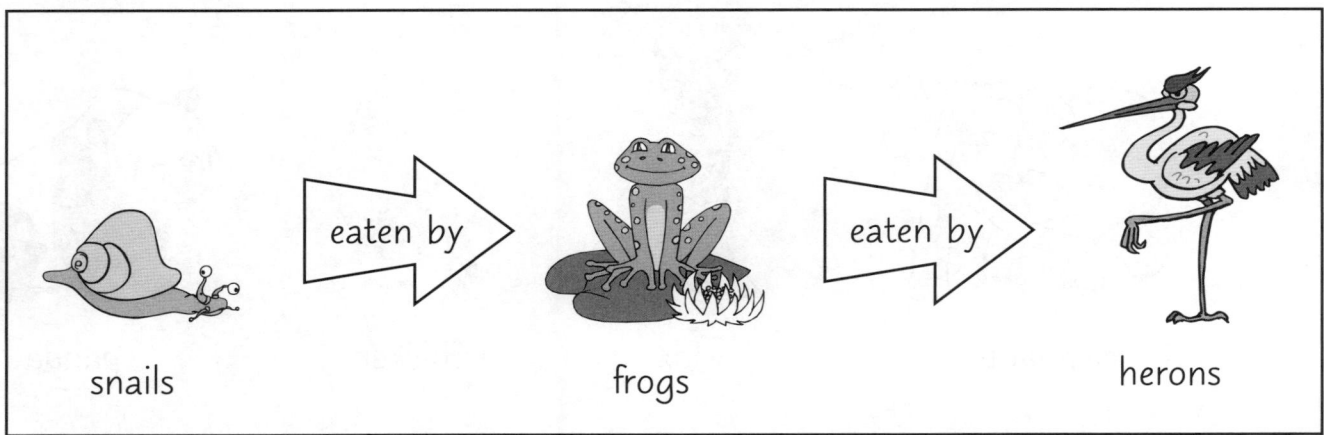

What animal do **frogs eat**?

....

What animal **eats frogs**?

....

7. Fill in the food chain for **penguins**, **fish** and **sharks**.

.... ⇨ .... ⇨ ....

What Eats What?

Here is another food chain.

leaves   caterpillars   squirrels   hawks

8. Finish these sentences about **this food chain**.

> Caterpillars eat ....
>
> Caterpillars are eaten by ....
>
> Squirrels are eaten by ....
>
> Nothing eats ....

9. Which of these animals also **eats leaves**? Tick (✔) your answer.

     ☐ sharks   ☐ pigeons   ☐ slugs

10. Which of these animals do **hawks** also **eat**? Tick (✔) your answer.

     ☐ horses   ☐ mice   ☐ cows

INVESTIGATE

People are part of lots of food chains too. Draw the food chain for someone eating beef, and someone eating chicken. Remember to put what the animals eat in your food chain. Can you draw a food chain for anything else you eat?

Mixed Questions

1. Look at the objects.

Draw a **green** circle around the things that **are alive**.

Draw a **red** circle around the things that **used to be alive**.

Draw a **blue** circle around the things that **were never alive**.

Mixed Questions

2. What is a habitat? Put a tick (✔) next to your answer.

   ☐ the place where a plant or animal lives

   ☐ the clothes a nun wears

   ☐ a picture showing what eats what

3. Match the plant or animal to where it **lives**. One has been done for you.

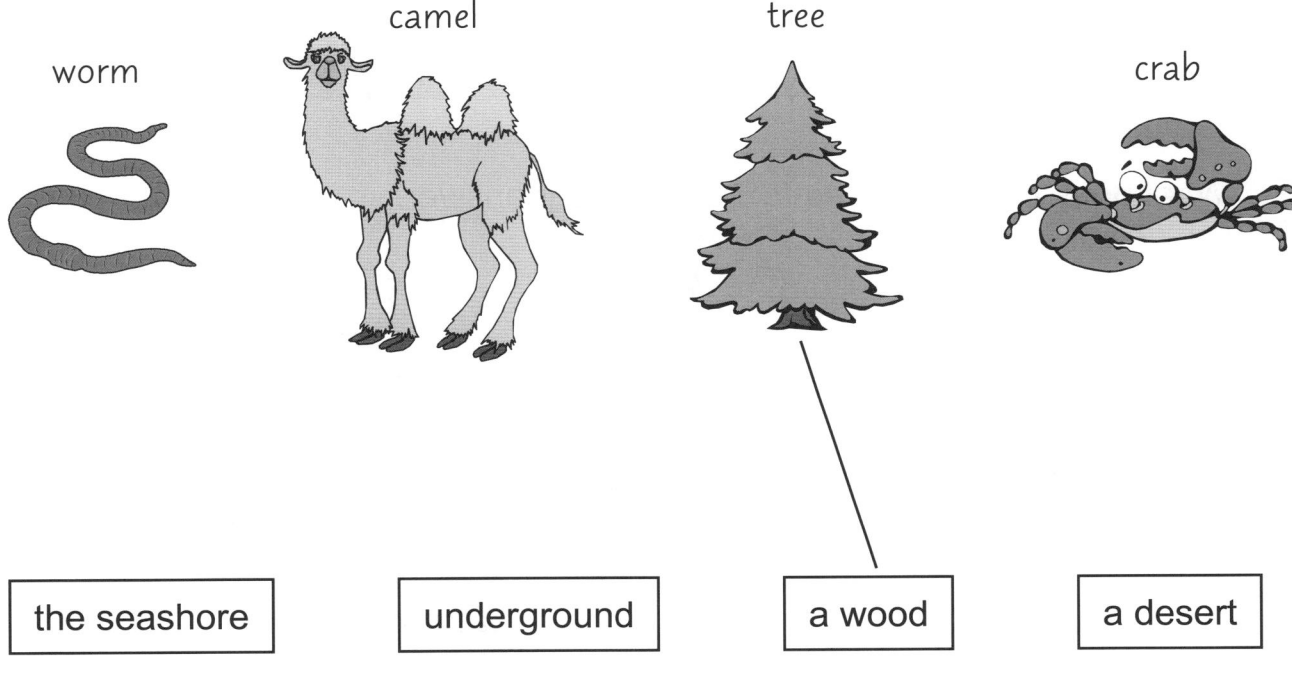

| the seashore | underground | a wood | a desert |

4. Draw a ⓒircle around all of the **micro-habitats**. You need to draw **three** circles.

   | **under a rock** | **a forest** | **an old log** |

   | **a meadow** | **a rock pool** | **the sea** |

Mixed Questions

This is a picture of a grassy habitat in **Africa**.

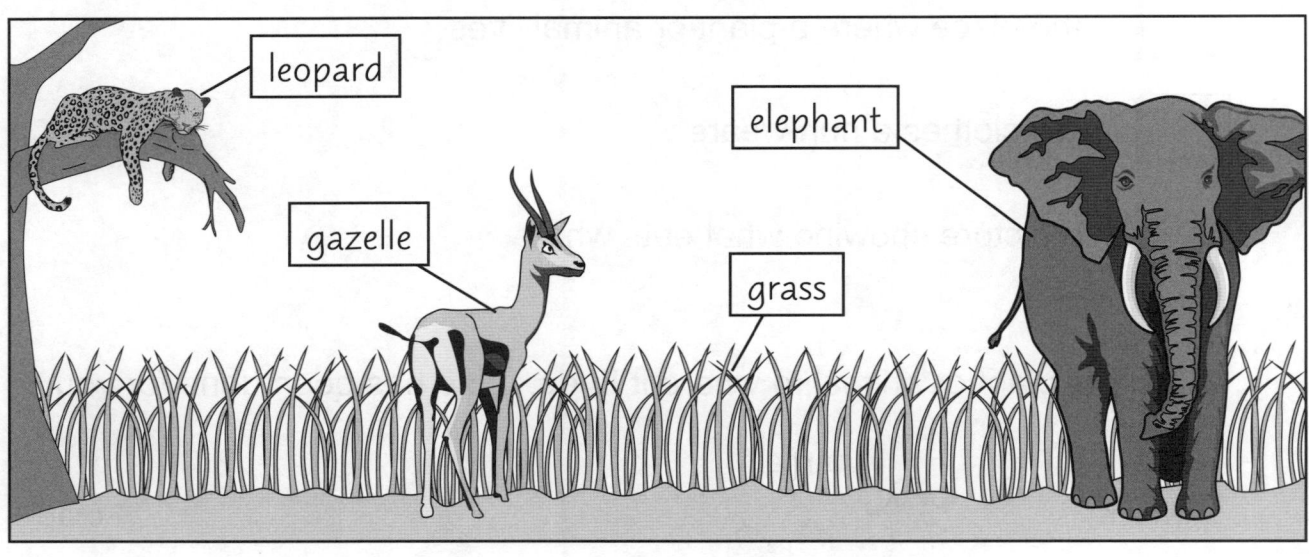

5. What does the **gazelle** eat? Tick (✔) your answer.

   ☐ leopards   ☐ grass   ☐ elephants

6. The leopard is a **carnivore**. It eats **gazelles**.
   What does the leopard use the **grass** for? Circle your answer.

   to hide in when it is trying to catch gazelles

   for food

   to build a nest

7. Finish the **food chain** for the **grass**, the **gazelle**, and the **leopard**.

   .... ⇨ ......gazelle...... ⇨ ....

Mixed Questions

8. Answer the questions about **this food chain**.

What eats the **hedgehog**?

....

What eats the **lettuce**?

....

What does the **hedgehog eat**?

....

Does anything eat the **badger**?

....

9. **Rabbits** eat lettuce. **Foxes** eat rabbits.
Draw a food chain for rabbits, lettuce and foxes.

Glossary

Amphibian	Amphibians spend part of their lives in water and part of their lives on land. **Frogs**, **toads** and **newts** are amphibians.
Carnivore	An animal that only eats **meat**.
Desert	An area that's very **dry**. Lots of deserts are also very **hot**. This means that only a few things can live there, like **cactuses** and **camels**.
Food chain	Food chains show what **eats** what. For example, the food chain for **mice** eating **grain** and **cats** eating **mice** looks like this: grain ⟶ mice ⟶ cats.
Habitat	A plant or animal's habitat is where it **usually lives**, like a pond.
Mammal	Most mammals are **furry**. They **give birth** instead of laying eggs. Cats, dogs and bears are all mammals.
Meadow	A **grassy** area.
Micro-habitat	A **small habitat**. It could be a **pile of leaves** or under a **rock** or a **log**.
Nest	**Birds** make nests from grass, twigs, and other things they can find. Birds lay their **eggs** in nests.
Rainforest	A forest where it **rains** a lot. **Tropical rainforests** are also very **warm**. Lots of **different** kinds of **plants** and **animals** live in tropical rainforests.